HORSE WISE

HORSE WISE

Thinking Outside the Stall
and Other Lessons
I Learned from My Horse

CHERYL KIMBALL

CONARI PRESS

First published in 2004 by Conari Press,
an imprint of Red Wheel/Weiser, LLC
York Beach, ME
With offices at:
368 Congress Street
Boston, MA 02210
www.redwheelweiser.com

LIBRARY OF CONGRESS CATALOGING-IN-PUBLICATION DATA
Kimball, Cheryl.
  Horse wise : thinking outside the stall and other lessons I learned
from my horse / Cheryl Kimball.
    p. cm.
  ISBN 1-57324-866-5 (alk. paper)
  1. Conduct of life. 2. Horses—Psychology—Miscellanea. I. Title.
BF637.C5K55 2004
158.1—dc22

                        2003024984

Typeset in Perpetua by Kathleen Wilson Fivel
"Cowboy" (owned by Jerry McClare in Maine) illustration by Karmel Timmons
Printed in Canada
TCP

11 10 09 08 07 06 05 04
  8 7 6 5 4 3 2 1

This book is dedicated to all horses, but especially the five horses who currently share my home: Bud, Ruby, Cleo, Willy, and Bugsy. They provide me with motivation, inspiration, patience, confidence, and whatever wisdom I might possess. Quite simply, horses infuse joy and wonder into every single one of my days and I am willing to forever try to live up to such a gift.

Contents

———◆◆◆———

Introduction

As a child I had a collection of model horses and played horse on the elementary school playground, but it wasn't until I was fifteen that I became involved with *real* horses. My best friend's boyfriend's sister had horses in her backyard; when Karen and I proved ourselves responsible teenagers, Pat was happy to get her horses exercised during a time when she was busy taking care of her little girl.

In my early twenties I got a horse of my own. I named her Cheka, which I had read was Swahili for "smiling." She was a young buckskin-colored Quarter Horse filly that I purchased for $500. We had two years of fun and frustration before a boyfriend and job took priority and I ended up selling her.

Thirteen years passed before I got into horses again.

When I did, now in my early thirties, I bought another youngster, this time a gelding named Bud, at a bargain basement price. My intention was for us to learn together. While this is a great strategy with puppies, it isn't always the best plan with horses. If you don't know how to educate a horse—and I certainly had not gained that knowledge in the years of my equine hiatus—it is just as likely to be a dangerous situation as a learning experience. My early years with Bud turned out to be both.

To my great fortune, a few months after my purchase, I caught on to a style of horsemanship that changed my life. It was an approach that was interested in *educating* horses, not training them; that believed in allowing and encouraging horses to think while still expecting respect from them. At first I thought I was lucky to have stumbled upon this approach so soon after my re-entry to the horse world. But on reflection, I didn't merely stumble upon this, I was actively looking for it—I just didn't know what *it* was. I had vowed that my new horse life would be different from my last experience or I was done with horses. By opening myself up to the wisdom I could learn from horses, I learned many great life lessons— lessons that I'd like to share with you in this book.

When my first horse, Cheka, wouldn't go in the

trailer, for instance, I had absolutely no idea how to teach her to load in—I would simply try to make her until we were both angry and frustrated. An hour or so and a couple of extra people later, she would be on the trailer, though neither of us was feeling very good about our relationship. If you have never tried to force a 1,000-pound animal whose instincts and decisions revolve around not being some other animal's dinner to do something they don't want to do—well, let's just say that a 125-pound human ultimately can't make a horse do anything. Oh, people appear to do it all the time, and the horse is a very accommodating creature for the most part; with a few exceptions, a horse really just wants to get along with the least amount of stress and fuss possible. Isn't that pretty much what we all want? To get through life with as little stress possible? But the minute horses decide not to be accommodating, watch out. Self-preservation is a strong thing in prey animals and to watch this instinct take over a horse's mind is a sight to behold.

Some of what I learned when I discovered this new approach to horses is that not only is it futile to try to make a horse do anything—it is gratifying to learn how to teach a horse in a way that makes sense to the horse. How, to use a phrase coined by master horseman, Ray Hunt, "to make your idea the horse's idea." (Take note, parents, it works with kids, too. And husbands, wives, bosses....) My horse life, and as a result my entire life, changed in the moment that I saw that this was possible.

It took a few years for me to realize the lessons I was learning from my horse. This is not something you *get* overnight. Over those years, however, I began to develop the tools I needed in my toolbox to call upon when situations arise. I began to know how to expect and ask for respect (and how to give respect to a horse) as well as softness and yielding from my horses and, most importantly, how to direct their feet.

I learned that the reins are attached to the bit, which is physically in the horse's mouth but is really attached to the feet, all of which is ultimately attached to the horse's mind. If you get to the mind, you will get to the feet, and the feet are what you need to do everything you want to do with the horse—go left, back up, avoid that rock in the trail, take a right turn down another trail, get out of that other rider's way, get out of the corral without letting the herd out, even stand still to be brushed. After all, to have them in the barn aisle and brush them you need them to stand still, right? If you have been around horses, you may think, "not really, there are these things called cross ties." Cross ties are lead ropes attached to either side of the barn aisle which you attach to either side of the horse's halter—and *make* the horse stand still.

And so we get back to that "make" thing again—it is ultimately more efficient and feels better for both horse and rider if you don't try to make a horse do anything. If you teach the horse that when he has a halter and lead rope on he does not move his feet unless you request him to, well, when there is no pressure at all on the lead rope, he simply stands still. Then you don't have to try to make it happen.

Confinement to a horse is the worst thing imaginable. Horses' brains are hardwired to flee at danger. What horses perceive as danger is sometimes puzzling to humans, although that is the topic for a whole book itself. Suffice it to say that it seems apparent that if a horse feels trapped, all he seems to think about is moving. If he feels that he could move if he really needed to, he seems much more able to stand still. (I did not dream this up myself. Many of the clinicians I have studied with have pointed this out.)

Humans, even the most *upper-level* equestrians, spend a lot of time confining their horses—putting them in stalls and on cross ties for the convenience of the human, using bigger and harsher bits to "gain more control," forcing their mouths shut with tight nosebands, and using a piece of equipment called a "tiedown" or "martingale" to keep his head at the desired height while riding (referred to in horse circles as forcing the horse "into a frame" or creating a "head set").

Once I learned that the key to being safe and avoiding frustration around horses means learning to direct their feet, I had the fundamental tool I needed to start to relax. This is where my horse life took a sharp turn. If you know how to direct a horse's feet and how teach the horse what you are looking for, you become more interested in encouraging the horse's freedom of movement than confining the horse. There are a lot of riders who think they are encouraging freedom in the horse, but it is freedom under the rider's terms. If you know how to direct the feet, you can allow the horse freedom under the horse's terms—only you are doing the directing.

This new horse life continued gradually to transcend my life. The knowledge I gained—keep it simple, learn to think differently, lead through respect not dominance, consider the horse's perspective—affected my overall way of being. This knowledge provided me with some new tools to do things like be a manager in a company and provide leadership to other employees especially in times of turmoil. I feel comfortable moving into middle age with some knowledge behind me that, if I use it wisely, will enable me to continue to expand those boundary lines. While the inclination has always been there, that knowledge has been gained through a quest for good horsemanship, by learning through my interactions with horses. And that is what the rest of this book is about.

Open-Minded Doesn't Mean "Sucker for Anything"

I had always considered myself open-minded. But I hadn't really thought much about what that meant until someone suggested I was close-minded when it came to horsemanship.

On a damp March day in 1991, I took a riding lesson at a local stable. I was looking for something physical and animal-related to add to my life. The lesson was entertaining but not compelling enough to draw me back.

Two months later I stopped by a former riding buddy's place. The first thing she asked when I walked up to the door was "you wanna buy a horse?" I chuckled but throughout our visit her question stuck in my mind like a dream that you can't quite shake. *Do* I want to buy a horse? My friend, a great salesperson, even saddled up a couple of her riding horses and we went for a short ride.

The rhythmic clip-clop of the horses' feet plopping along the back road was relaxing, and it was refreshing to be outside in the waning sun of a spring afternoon. When we finished, I took another peek at the horse for sale.

That week, I found myself doing some research about the current expenses of owning a horse. Then I did some soul-searching. Did I really want the responsibility of a horse? Was I willing to add commuting to a boarding barn to my schedule? I had a pretty cushy lifestyle; did I really want to shake it up? I guess so. Within a month, Bud was mine.

The key to my plan, however, was that my new life with horses would be different from my old life with horses. There were many things about that former horse world that I did not like. The frustration, for instance, of getting a horse to stand for the horseshoer. The way horses bring out my lack of patience, especially when I need to do something like load them in a trailer. And especially the dreaded chain lead rope.

One way that many horse people use to attempt to control horses when handling them is a lead rope with a several-inch chain on the end that wraps around the delicate part of the horse's nose before clipping to the other side of the halter. This chain, when snapped, is supposed to add some control. It always makes me cringe, though; I suspect it damages the horse's nose, and it's questionable whether or not any real control is gained with this chain. But I had used one of these chains on my first horse, and I used one for the first few months I had my new horse, simply because I had no idea what else to do. That was, until I signed up for a clinic on starting a young horse under saddle that changed and saved my horse life.

The clinician presented to the two dozen or so participants and a couple hundred spectators a way of handling horses that worked with the horse's natural instincts to make teaching things and presenting new things to the horse easier for both horse and handler. A horse's instincts are many—the supreme concern with self-preservation, the need to flee perceived danger, and the strong preference to get along, expend as little energy as necessary, and avoid confusion and chaos as much as possible.

This clinic taught me to work with the horse where it is at, use the horse's natural instincts when you can, and try to open the door to the response you want from the horse and shut the door to the response you don't want. And the tools you need are simple: a halter, lead rope, bridle, a saddle, and an open mind.

For several years, I hung around only with other like-minded individuals. However, I have never been much of a group person, so when I felt like I had some basic skills down and that I had reasonable control of my horse's feet, I ventured out into the greater horse world and rode with people outside of my circle. And this is where I encountered the idea that I was not very open-minded about horsemanship. And, you know what, it's still probably true.

The horse world is full of gimmicks—reins with elastic ends that give for you instead of the rider having to learn to give, different bits with little gimmicks that are said to work miracles to change behavior, training methods that involve clickers and treats. I have never denied that any of these things work—they sure do. But I adamantly believe that using these gimmicks does not represent good horsemanship. I believe that many of them skirt around hard work and make a mockery of the horse. The horse is an incredible animal that is willing to interact with the likes of humans. I believe those of us who choose to interact with horses (it is certainly not the horse making that choice!) are obligated to treat them with respect—which includes expecting them to treat us with respect.

And so I remain somewhat close-minded, I guess, in that I have found one way of working with horses that gives me criteria to use in assessing other methods, and it has served me well so far. I've saved a bundle of money not buying the gimmicks. And I'm dedicated to the idea that to have deeper relationships, you need to do the hard work, to get beyond the physical, beyond appearances. But I've come to realize that I am also open-minded in the sense that although everything I do when I work with a new horse has to fit into a certain criteria, I am open to all sorts of things within those parameters. If something doesn't work, I try something else—that fits within my criteria. And that holds true with every aspect of my life, whether it is spirituality, business, or just watching television.

Anger and a Half-Ton Horse

------◆------

Getting angry with a horse is like trying to fight a forest fire with a squirt gun—there is no question you are outpowered. A horse's reaction to human anger goes in a couple directions: she gets defensive or she gives up in defeat. The first is something you probably don't want to experience, the second is downright depressing.

For the everyday horse owner, anger often arises when we can't get a horse to do something we want her to do—stand still while the farrier works on her feet, go through a puddle, get in a trailer, stand to be mounted, stop grazing along the trail. Even aged horses who have been taught the behaviors we *want* them to have do not necessarily continue with them when they come into the hands of someone who does not know how to expect these things from the horse. Horses will always, almost without exception, work their way up or down to the level of their handler/rider. The less-skilled rider would do well to up his or her skill level. Novice horse owners often think that horses should simply understand these things. Many times they simply don't know what to do to help the horse understand, which leads them both along the ugly trail from frustration to anger.

When we get angry, our horses seem to get fearful. Something about anger in one being seems to bring out fear in other beings. Despite the psychobabble about how anger can be a good thing, in my experience anger rarely, if ever, comes from a good place or has anywhere good to go (except perhaps to loosen frozen lug nuts on a flat tire when you are perched on the shoulder of a dark road).

I don't believe horses return anger in response to anger. I believe that they get confused when their handler is angry simply because they don't understand what the human is asking of them. An angry human can be very unclear to a horse—anger steals the preciseness of our timing and consistency, two essential keys to a horse's comprehension, and offers up only confusion.

A horse who perceives danger in your anger will

become defensive—if you provoke a horse to the point where that natural self-preservation instinct steps in, he will strike out with his front legs, swing his rear at you and kick, or even lunge with teeth bared. None of which is any fun to be on the receiving end of.

He doesn't care if you are the person who has fed him every day twice a day for two years or has brushed him or lovingly cared for him when he was sick or injured. Self-preservation in the prey animal trumps all. If you are his caretaker, it may take quite a bit more pressure for that self-preservation to kick in, but when it does the horse is not analyzing who you are and how many times in the past you have been nice to him—horses live in the moment, and moments that call for self-preservation draw upon every defense the horse has.

The horse who responds in defeat to constant anger is a sad, depressing sight. Most animals, especially prey animals, have a built-in mechanism that shuts down their senses in order to not suffer physically. As a result, of course, they suffer mentally and become disengaged with the world around them.

But physical abuse is far from the only way a horse can be abused. I would go out on a limb and say that most abused horses are not extremely physically mistreated but mentally abused—they are not beaten and their lives are not threatened, but they are always in a state of worry about where that next sharp spur or stinging whip or jabbing bit is going to come in. They may be drilled and drilled and drilled with "schooling" to compete in a horse show. The horse doesn't care about this but, in their get-along kind of way, many horses tolerate this drilling day after day after day. They do this by checking out mentally and just going along physically with what their handler wants them to do. I think we all can recall feeling like this in school!

In the right hands, a mentally abused horse can be rehabilitated but many just check out for life. The kindest thing may be to let him simply hang out in peace for the rest of his days; the very least you can do is give the horse something else to do than what he was doing, something to give the horse purpose in life.

When I attended my first horse clinic at age thirty-four, I got pretty angry with my young horse as I tried to do the things the clinician showed us. Despite my good intentions, my horse was running me over and paying no attention to me at all. No, I wasn't beating him, but I was clearly angry with the horse. And I wasn't the only one. I heard the clinician say, "I see some of you have the ability to get pretty angry with your horses. I could have some fun with that." I could envision him giving us more and more complicated things to do until my horse and I were wound up into a red hot fireball.

I was quite certain the clinician meant that if he "had fun" with my anger with my horse, our tasks wouldn't get any easier—and I wasn't having much fun to begin with! From that moment on, I attempted to control my anger—that's not to say that it hasn't surfaced over the years, but I am aware of it and can more quickly get it in check. And the more I learn about effective teaching, the less I find anger arises—not only with horses but in my whole life. It starts to go back to that "make the right thing easy" concept—if you work on trying to open the right doors, anger doesn't have to arise. For instance, instead of arguing with your husband about the house being dirty, talk through the ways you can both contribute to keeping the house neater. Not getting to anger in the first place paves a smoother way.

Create the Life You Want

A friend recently told me about the difficulties she and her boyfriend were experiencing in their relationship. She thought they were on the verge of breaking up. I commented that, judging from the times we had spent together, their relationship seemed worth working on. And I said that after nineteen years with my husband, I knew that it is possible to have a comfortable, non-tumultuous relationship. My friend replied, "You're lucky."

Yes, I suppose there is some luck involved. I feel fortunate and grateful for our life together, but nineteen years of a strong relationship comes from a lot of hard work, not luck.

In order to have the life you want, you first need to know what that life is, then you need to create it.

Step by step. Creating your life is hard work. It's easy to get off track or to start to think you want a different kind of thing than what suits you. It's also a lot easier to give up on the life you want and simply settle for the life you get.

My horses helped me create the kind of lifestyle I have always wanted. First, having horses got me to work toward having a suitable home where I could keep them myself. That led to the purchase of our ninety-acre farm. This was not a home choice that came out of the blue. When I was a kid, we drove several times each summer to our camp on a lake. Along the country roads that wound their way to our camp, I would gaze longingly out the window at the farm houses we passed—sturdy barns, porches, beds of flowers hugging the foundations. My cousin lived in a place such as this. I loved to visit her and her brothers and their pony. The farm we bought when I was thirty-six years old was like buying a piece of the childhood of my imagination.

Because horses require a considerable amount of time—at least two hours a day maintenance if I don't want to be buried in manure, plus whatever riding time I am willing to give them—I tend to be home a lot. When you have a ninety-acre place with riding trails and a lake with a semi-private beach around the corner, staying home is not a hardship.

In order to be able to fit in that two hours of maintenance and ride, I decided I needed to be able to work from home. I now work from my office in the carriage house writing and editing books. This was not something that happened overnight—it was only after several years commuting to jobs in the book publishing industry and writing dozens of articles at night and on weekends that I was able to mount a successful freelance career.

Working at home itself requires an immense amount of discipline. I need to sit at my computer if I have a deadline, even if the sun is pouring in my windows, begging me to come outside. I need to market myself. I've had to write books on topics I wasn't necessarily passionate about in less time than I would have preferred in order to build relationships and get future work—and to pay that old nag, the mortgage. And sometimes those books led to dead ends. No relationship was built as intended, and I had to work hard not to get discouraged. In a roundabout way, my horses also taught me persistence.

Through it all, I had a general plan. I have deviated from the plan several times, and I alter the plan as my career and interests mature and change. But the horses in the barn offer a framework for my life and my lifestyle.

And sometimes divergences are thrown in the way—illness, death, tragedy, or an opportunity that can't be passed up but doesn't really fit the master plan—and you need to draw on your imagination to continue to create the life you want within that divergence.

I am often asked how I can stand being so "tied down." It's as if people think I've accumulated horses without realizing it or against my will. I created this life, it didn't just happen. I knew exactly how I wanted to live, and I went about creating it. And whenever I walk into the corral and interact with my horses—which is every single day—I realize how important this interaction is to me, how privileged I feel to be comfortable around horses. If I wanted my life to be different, I would work at creating a different life.

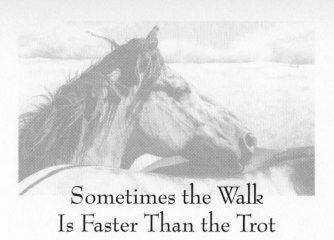

Sometimes the Walk
Is Faster Than the Trot

A concept that is emphasized by a lot of clinicians I study with is "sometimes going slow is the fastest way to accomplish what you want." The horses themselves have proven it time and again.

Time is a human invention. Horses use time as well, but their concept of time is dictated by an interior clock, not by an artificial one tacked to the wall. While hunger pangs and the physiological need for the equine digestive system to have food constantly traveling through it control "feed time," my horses also seem to have certain times when they settle in a patch of sun or shade, cock a leg, take a nap, or head over the hill to check out the grazing possibilities there. They don't need a clock on the wall to tell them to do these things, their inner clock knows. We humans have inner clocks, too. Our challenge is to listen to our inner clock more often instead of getting hung up on the one on the wall.

Many times people try to teach a horse something—as small as a specific maneuver to as grand as saddling them and riding them for the first time—with the pressure of time bearing down on them. A classic scenario for getting a young horse "broke to ride" is to send her to a professional horse trainer who typically has organized her or his business around a "ninety-day program"—a program designed for the expediency of making money, not for the good of the horse. At the end of three months, your young horse comes back ready to ride, show, and whatever else you have planned for her. If a horse doesn't fit a trainer's ninety-day program, it is often condemned as dumb or unathletic or even a rogue and accompanied by the recommendation to sell the horse and get a more suitable one.

The best trainer is willing to abandon "the program" and work with the horse as an individual creating a goal for a particular lesson and taking whatever time is needed to accomplish that goal—or even changing the goal if something else comes up. How many times have you tried to fit something into an artificial timeframe? Maybe it's dieting, maybe it's writing a book or teaching your child golf. Unfortunately, we can't avoid time constraints but when we let things take the time they need we avoid spending more time *fixing* things later.

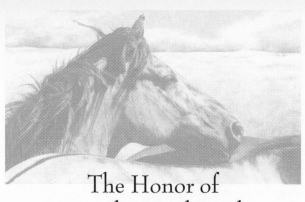

The Honor of
Being the Herd Leader

Horses live in a social hierarchy—as do humans —but horses don't mind. In fact, they take comfort in it.

The social existence of a horse is dictated by herd hierarchy. Horses look to a leader to help them get through the day. The herd leader is typically a mare— she decides when the herd will move and to where. The stallion is the protector of the herd but when his protective role is unnecessary, he follows the mare's lead. While all members of the herd are under the leadership of the mare, each horse in the herd, depending on her place on the hierarchical ladder, has one or more other leaders to follow as well.

When a human chooses to take a horse under her or his care, the specific social dynamics change considerably, but ultimately that horse is still looking for a leader. Horses do not seem to like being adrift without hierarchy. If the horse doesn't find that leader in her human caretaker, she will take on the leadership role herself. Horses seem to clearly feel, to again paraphrase one of the world's best contemporary horsemen, Ray Hunt, that "someone has to run this outfit." If it's not going to be the human member of the team, it's going to be the horse.

This is where many horse owners get in trouble. They approach leadership as a negative concept focused on dominance and intimidation with the intention of creating fear in those being led. This is not leadership, this is dictatorship.

In a National Public Radio report on the 2002 retirement of Boston Pops conductor Seiji Ozawa, a member of the Pops orchestra was asked what it was like playing for Ozawa. She said it was like dancing with a man who was a great dancer—a real leader who never made you wonder where you were supposed to put your feet.

A horse with a great conductor either on the end of the lead rope or in the saddle never has to wonder where to put her feet either. A rider who is a leader to the horse, who considers the reins connected not to the horse's mouth but to her feet, will inspire and reassure almost any horse. Inspiration and reassurance do not come through dominance and coercion.

I have always considered taking on a leadership role to be a great honor and responsibility both in my various publishing jobs and with my horses. Leaders do not leave people wondering what to do next; they give them the tools they need to make good decisions and to be able to proceed with confidence. A good leader also lets people flounder around a little, searching for their own path to the answer they need—all the while knowing the leader is there, aware of the situation and ready to step in and reassure or clarify when necessary.

Dominance is often mistaken for leadership. When I first got my big strong gelding, a farrier came to trim his hooves. I was holding the lead rope while the farrier did his work, and on the last foot my horse snatched his hoof out of the farrier's hand. The farrier, someone I'd known for a while, took the opportunity to take the horse from me and teach us a lesson. He thrashed my horse around the barn and when he was done, my horse practically saluted him. He was right. I needed that lesson. But the lesson I got wasn't the one he thought he was teaching.

The farrier's method didn't impress me one bit—in fact, it made me decide right then and there that if I couldn't get that kind of reaction from my horse without that kind of negative experience, then horses were not what I was interested in. Not only did I not want to thrash my horse around the barn, I didn't have it in me to do that.

Later, someone who became a mentor to me explained what had happened. I told her about the incident and how I really wanted my horse to be that attentive to me but I didn't want to accomplish it in that way. She explained that the farrier had gotten the horse's attention through fear, not through respect. It is the Trojan Horse of horsemanship—by using that kind of method you can get the horse to give you what you want, but inside the horse there is a whole lot of negativity going on. My horse told me that at the time; I could feel it, but I didn't know what it was I was seeing and feeling. I just knew it looked like what I wanted but it wasn't.

A good leader gains his or her role through respect. You can lead through dominance and fear, but that only creates negative feelings. Leadership through respect creates good feelings all around.

The Importance of
Having a Source of Peace

My high school friend, Karen, and I would race to the barn after school and by three o'clock in the afternoon we were horseback and halfway to the Atlantic Ocean, just a mile away. If the tide was low we would play around on the ocean's edge, leaving hoof prints in the sand as evidence of our fun. If the tide was high, we would walk along the edge and cross over the beach rocks to ride the dirt road on "the island," the smooth grey beach stones tumbling and crunching under the horses' feet. We entered the island road at a sharp corner around which was a straightaway well known to the horses as the place we galloped; by the time we turned the corner, our horses, Breezy and Alana, were ready to run, prancing and crowhopping like they knew the excitement of a starting gate at the racetrack.

Off we went, never worrying about how fast we were going because we knew that when we got to the end of the straightaway where the abandoned cement military lookout tower loomed (now serving not much more purpose than stopping a couple fast horses), Breeze and Lani would automatically slow down just like they automatically got revved up at the beginning.

Karen's horse, a tall grey Thoroughbred/Arabian cross, was always much faster than my mount, an aging chestnut Quarter Horse gelding. I admired Karen for how brave she was to ride the powerful grey horse; I was a timid rider and grateful to have a kind, forgiving horse to ride. Our married friend who owned the horses had come to trust us so much that I was given permission to ride Breezy whenever I wanted to. I lived less than a mile from her and for a couple years that horse became my source of entertainment and my source of comfort.

One Christmas Day shortly after my boyfriend, who was several years older than I was, had dumped me for the excitement of a woman more his age, I managed to open presents with my family, eat some part of Christmas dinner, then bundled up and went to saddle up Breezy. He didn't know it was Christmas, it was just another ride. We plodded down the road to the beach, snowflakes melting on us as they landed.

The air was heavy with the moist weight of the ocean. We walked the entire way to the beach; I was in no hurry to get back to my misery. We trotted around the beach at the edge of the churning surf which was making that soothing swooshing sound as it spread itself out across the sand, then collected itself back again. I will never forget the entire ride. Although I felt no better when I got back to the real world, I certainly felt better while riding.

Now I find that place of peace in several ways. It may be sitting on my mare at the top of the hill on our property next to the cemetery and taking the place in after a nice trail ride. It may be curled up on the couch with a book in my hand and a dog at my feet. Sometimes just thinking about those peaceful moments can help me relax. I highly recommend finding places like this of your own—maybe it's a rocky mountaintop, maybe it's in the video arcade, maybe it's in the car. It doesn't matter as long as it works for you.

Equine Tutorials

S oon after my miserable first year at college, I decided to get my own horse. Cheka was a young buckskin Quarter Horse. She was small and cute and in my price range, and she was only three years old. Her current owner, whose brother had gotten the horse as a gift but really didn't want her, had saddled her once so I just assumed she was "rideable." And she was *rideable* but she sure didn't know much about being ridden. And I didn't know much about educating her either.

Considering her lack of education, she took good care of me for the two years I had her. She and I even won blue ribbons at judged trail rides. But despite our good times, there were bad times as well. She was difficult to load in a trailer. We had a tremendous fight at a wooden bridge she refused to go over, and she was not too tolerant of the farrier.

The good moments were a lot of fun but the bad moments were so frustrating that after two years I sold her. My mind was on a new job with a bit of a commute and a new boyfriend who occupied my weekends. Looking back, I realize I simply was not ready for the lessons she could have taught me. Maybe there have been times in your life when you have given up just before your teacher arrived. The lesson may still be ahead of you like it was for me.

The horse I bought a decade later was a two-year-old who had never been saddled and ridden. Somewhere in those ten years, I began to learn that when it came to things like horses, you didn't just bump up against them, you took them on as a responsibility. The quality of my horse's life depended on me. My new horse was not going to spend his life with a nose chain, whips, and gimmicks. If I couldn't figure out how to have that happen, then he could spend his life with someone else.

I took Bud to a clinic I saw advertised in a horse publication. It was nearby, it sounded intriguing, and it claimed that I would have my horse started under saddle over the course of the five days.

At that clinic were my teachers—two people and

my horse—all of whom were to become what I needed to have this horse be a catalyst in a life-changing refinement of my own way of being. They could have had flashing neon lights on them and not been more evident. One of them was the owner of the stable where the clinic took place. During the clinic, I managed to convince her to let me move my new horse to her boarding stable, even though she didn't have much room left and I had to commute fifty miles each way to get there.

The other human teacher in the building that day was the clinician. Although the clinic was only five days long and he disappeared back to the west where he had come from, I knew by the end of the first day of the clinic that this guy held the key to a very important door. In the years since, I have attended a couple dozen of his clinics all over the country, either as a spectator or a participant. I may not be his most talented student but I certainly am one of the most dedicated. The door was wide open and someday I hope to take the hinges off all together.

The lessons have not been easy. I have spent thousands of dollars on my horse education, traveled hundreds of miles, gotten up many mornings at five A.M. to tend to the rest of my horses before hurrying off to get to the clinic site to feed the horse I had there. I've ridden in clinics in the blistering heat and the frigid cold, and with hips so painful the next thing out of me was going to be tears (thank goodness the latter issue has gotten better through chiropractics, stretching, and Feldenkrais Therapy). I've fallen off, not been able to accomplish what I was being shown to do, and worried that I was ruining my horses. But I've had fleeting moments of the often elusive quest in horsemanship called "unity," and those moments were pure enough to keep me searching for more. I learned in that first clinic that I was the student, the horse was simply the project I used to work on me. Although many people will point to the horse as the *problem* it is the human that needs to change in order for the horse to change.

I was so ready for my teachers and their lessons, it was like they had conference name tags on them— "Hello, My Name Is Cheryl's Teacher." I absorbed their lessons like a Bounty paper towel. And these teachers were so good that they knew how to send me off on my own—and taught me to recognize when I might need to come back for a refresher course.

I think it's the chicken-and-the-egg thing: you need to know what the lesson is you want before the teachers you need appear, but you need the teachers to present the lesson before you know that's the lesson you want. Be on the lookout for your own teachers—they may be right in front of you or just around the next corner!

Learn About How You Learn

Some people learn best by allegory—by being told a story that represents an example of the point being made. Other people learn by having something demonstrated to them. Others can learn something more easily once they get a chance to do it themselves. Some people can learn quite well from a book using step-by-step instructions, while others need to read the theory behind the lesson before it makes sense.

Attending horse clinics has helped me discover a lot about my own learning style. One of the significant things I've discovered is that I need different teaching styles under different circumstances. When I bring a young, busy horse to a clinic, I'm looking to get my horse exposed to some controlled chaos with guidance readily available but not where I am the center of attention such as in an individual lesson. When I work with my older mare at a clinic, I get the most out of a one-on-one or very small group situation where I can work on specific refinement.

But everyone doesn't fit into the same learning model. I have seen riders get completely lost in one situation and have a very successful learning experience in another. A friend who I'll call Jane is a very timid rider and needs lots of support while riding. Almost every move her horse makes causes her puzzlement, alarm, or celebration. Although it is a slow process, she is constantly attending clinics and always striving to improve. In a large group session, she simply does not get the support from the clinician that enables her to learn.

Jane signed up for one clinic where each day you got an individual session with the clinician. By the end of the third day, Jane was beaming with pride over the progress she made in her comfort level riding her new horse. She could listen to the clinician without the chaos of a group of riders swirling around her. But most of all, she could support her horse sufficiently in the more simple environment of a near-empty arena.

This isn't to say that this is the only way Jane will ever be able to take lessons with her horse. Your learning style may change throughout your life and through-out your progress mastering a certain skill. Like me with different horses, you may bounce back and forth as needed. Do you know how you learn best? For me, it took working with horses to think it through.

What horses add to the learning picture is an imme-diate barometer of whether or not you are learning what you want to learn. You don't have to wonder like we often do in our human communications ("Did she not say anything because she didn't like my work?" "Did he not mention my haircut because he doesn't like it?"). There's little subjectivity involved—you either have managed to explain clearly to your horse that when you hold your reins, legs, and body weight in a certain way you want a "leg yield" (to move her front legs on a different track than her back), or you haven't. Some horses just can't physically do some things and yes, like people, some are a little slower to learn than others.

A horse will let you know when you are frustrating him. I have one gelding who stresses out so badly when he is frustrated that he will simply attempt to flip you off like a cap on a cheap bottle of beer. His attempts are impressively sincere and his frustration level is almost immediate. He challenges me to make myself clearer while instructing him.

Horses learn "at the point of release." For instance, if you want a horse to learn to step back, you might pick up on the reins and put steady, same (not increasing) pressure on the reins. You release that pressure the second he moves back. As you increase your timing and awareness, you learn to release the pressure the second he simply rocks his weight back in preparation for moving, and then, when you get really good, for when he simply thinks about backing up.

If your timing is good enough to start right out with releasing at the "simply thinks about it" part, lucky you! After twelve years of trying I have just started to get to the point of knowing when the horse is preparing; I may have figured out my learning style, but I am still a slow learner....

Learning to be that aware is a useful life goal. Awareness can help you build better relationships with humans as well as horses. Awareness can help in every aspect of your life—from not falling down the stairs, to realizing a friend or family member is in trouble, to knowing your own limitations and needs and fulfilling them.

A Routine Isn't a Rut

I saw a quote once that said something like "taking a day off from a farm sets you back a week." Farm life imposes a routine that can become so ingrained that it is hard to break, even for a day.

Horse care can impose a strong routine as well. Many backyard horses are kept in small areas with little or no room to graze. They eat dry hay, not moist grass, and drink ten to fifteen gallons of water a day. And in order to make sure they have all the nutrients they need, our horses are fed grain, something they would never find in their natural environment. And the grains are often made to appeal as much to humans as horses, coated with molasses and mixed with this and that so they end up looking not unlike the granola we eat for breakfast. We feed horses all this in large allotments a couple times a day—quite different from the graze-and-roam way horses were created to eat. Often their feedings come in the morning before we go to work and in the evening when we get home.

It's important for a horse's digestive system to be processing food at all times. To accommodate that need, horse owners become fanatical about getting out to the barn at a certain hour in the morning and evening. I recall when I was working in an office forty-five minutes from home, I was careful to get out and do barn chores before I showered and got ready for work. At the end of the day, when my horses had gone for ten hours without a feeding, I often didn't even change my clothes when I returned home before I was in the barn dishing out hay.

Once you've established a routine like this with horses, they will practically tear the barn down if you are a couple minutes off schedule. My gelding antic-ipates feeding time and paces the fence line back and forth. One of my mares starts to paw the ground the minute I begin to clang the garbage cans that the grain is stored in. Stalled horses can really wreak havoc kick-ing walls and jumping around.

Most of this routine comes from good intention. We are anxious to re-create in however small a way the horse's natural eating needs. We break their daily ration up into at least two feedings so that their bodies do not have to consume all of the day's food at one time. And the more frequently they are fed throughout the day, the more they are busy with something natural like eating instead of pacing and pawing and being destructive.

How does routine fit into your life? Maybe it doesn't! My husband finds routine deadening. But I enjoy the way my horse-care routine sandwiches the day. I have a specific reason to get up early in the morning. And my routine shifts around some with the seasons. During the summer, I feed and clean stalls first thing; I like to get manure away from the barn before the flies wake up, and I like to feed early so the horses can be ready to be ridden before the heat of the day sets in.

In the winter, I make coffee and work at my desk until daylight. I feed and get the horses who are in stalls outside and I don't pick stalls and paddocks until noon when the sun is warmest. In winter, I also make a late evening trip to the barn filling water buckets and distributing some heat-generating hay to hold them over until daylight. This last trip to the barn energizes me to extend my own evening after I come in.

Of course, one of the great things about having a routine is breaking it! This helps my horses learn that they can be patient. Confined horses live a life of such relative boredom, that a little concern about when they might be getting fed gives them something to think about; the more you mix it up, the less restless they get in anticipation. And sometimes the guilty pleasure of lying in bed until 8 A.M. is just plain nice.

What routines do you have in your life? You may not think you have any, but you probably do—a muffin from the same shop every morning on the way to work, doing your laundry on the same day, even reading the same newspaper. Shake yourself up—break a routine and see how it feels.

Teach Respect for All Living Things

Over the years of my adulthood, I have surrounded myself with animals. First it was a dog. A couple years after that dog died of old age, my husband and I moved to the country with the specific intention of getting another dog. Then we got yet another dog. Then we bought a place with a forty-by-forty-foot barn. Now along with two dogs, I am caretaker to several horses, two goats, three barn cats, and until a year ago, several sheep.

One incident in particular that made me realize how much I love animals is a painful one to remember. But as I see it, we can learn important lessons from our mistakes. When I was a kid, my girlfriend, Alex, and I entertained ourselves much of the time exploring the woods around our houses. Besides climbing trees and investigating stonewalls, we were fascinated with a small pond a little way into the woods.

This pond was an oasis of cool in the heat of the pine forest. Its banks were soft with moss and hemlock needles, and the pond teemed with life including birds, bugs, and our personal favorite, frogs. We spent hours scouring this pond from one end to the other doing our own version of catch-and-release. One day we decided to capture some frogs in a couple of half-gallon milk jugs. The jugs were glass and had wide mouths—openings just big enough to stuff a frog through. We collected several frogs in each jug.

We had no intention of letting these frogs die; catch-and-release was always our modus operandi. We must have gotten distracted and forgot them or we underestimated or didn't understand how short a time period frogs can go without a lot of air. The jugs had water in them, but I suspect we screwed the lids on. Whatever the reason, all the frogs in the two jugs died. I feel awful to this day.

Horses continue to teach me to respect all living things. There is some controversy, for instance, in the horse world as to whether backyard horses are pets or livestock, and therefore, what constitutes adequate housing for them. I have a strong opinion about this.

Horses are large animals whose genetic makeup

revolves around lots of movement. They are not designed to be confined. If you confine them, then I believe it is your responsibility to get them so much exercise that they are exhausted and grateful when they get put back in their stall. Respect for a horse means giving them space to roam and exercise.

Horses not only like to roam, they *need* to roam. It is the core of their existence, and while their existence has evolved to be not much more than pleasuring humans, it doesn't mean we can't allow them some pleasure back. My own horses at this point do not have a lot of room relatively speaking—the five horses have maybe three acres—but they mostly have choice concerning moving around. While I separate them for the night to feed, they are still only locked in stalls for the most inclement weather; they may not have a lot of room to roam but they can walk around and trot and even run a little if they want to. Thinking of your own life, what happens to you when you are pent-up too much?

I believe that an insensitivity to animals is a precursor (or perhaps the indicator) of an insensitivity to other humans. I am not suggesting that those people who do not want to take on the responsibility of having an animal under their care learn to be insensitive— these people are realistic and practical and to be commended. In fact, they are being respectful by simply not taking on the care of an animal! But children should learn that animals are not dispensable— I cringe when I learn that an animal was euthanized because it became inconvenient.

Teach children to love and respect animals and you teach them a lifetime of caretaking and nurturing.

Maintain a Sense of Humor

One of the clinicians from whom I've learned a lot about horsemanship has a great sense of humor. While he's riding, he chuckles a lot at things the horse does in the process of learning. For a long time, I found that amazing—the horse he was riding would be doing everything imaginable to evade him or to search for the right answer and he would be up there in the saddle chuckling like he had a mini-television set in front of him with the comedy channel on.

But once I got beyond the intensity of the first few years of learning how to educate my horses, I also began to chuckle in the saddle. Riders who treat their horses like machines will never have that easy feeling.

Don't get me wrong, I'm not to the point where I get on my horse and everything is like a stand-up comedy routine (well, perhaps it is to the onlooker). I get frustrated and sometimes I even get cranky with my horse—the sort of "*what* are you doing?" kind of cranky. But more often than not, I find myself grinning and laughing at the things my horse does—for example when my mare tries to take over our partnership and do what she wants to do (like turning around and going back home to her herd). It has taken me over a decade to come to this point of humor in my horsemanship, but I feel it has made me become a better rider.

In my group of horse friends, there are a number of people who are totally serious and intense all the time. Many of them are awesome riders. If I have a question about something specific and technical about equitation, they are the people I ask. Most of them get beyond that intensity early on in a clinic. They lighten up and start to laugh and get a little more relaxed in the saddle instead of so technical. And when this happens, you can almost see their horses take a big sigh.

I think horses would laugh if they could. After listening to my many stories about my horses over the years, one of my colleagues in a previous job said, "I had no idea horses had such personality." That surprised me! If only everyone could get the chance to interact with horses and enjoy their personalities. They seem to do things for fun—they love to play. This can be a major horsemanship issue, especially with youngsters since you really don't want an eventual half-ton animal to think he can play with a 130-pound human. But there are ways to play with horses under the right circumstances.

Every winter, for instance, when we get the perfect snowball-making snowstorm, I go out into the horse pasture and build a snowman. I have to do this while the horses are eating some lunch hay or they won't leave me alone the whole time I am rolling the snowman's body segments. When I'm done stacking the three body parts, I stick in carrots for a nose and eyes and maybe ears too. I use some hay for hair and make a smile out of apples. And then I sit back and watch.

Before long, even if they haven't finished their hay, the horses investigate the snowman. Horses make this long low (and loud!) snort as they check out something that is strange to them. They all walk over to the snowman snorting, holding their heads low and snaking them around to get a full view and a good whiff. Because their eyes are on the sides of their heads, horses have significantly less binocular vision than humans—and they can see movement from very long distances for approximately 320 degrees around their bodies, although their ability to focus on what is moving at that distance isn't very sharp. The practical reason for this anatomical arrangement is, of course, that as prey animals, they can keep a good watch on things as they have their heads down grazing. It doesn't help them out much, though, when checking out a snowman.

After the horses decide the snowman is not a threat to them, they discover that it in fact holds treats for them. And when they do, watch out! Sometimes the snowman gets demolished as the dominant herd member does his level best to keep this snowman for himself. Other times, the snowman stays fairly intact while all the carrots and apples are eaten—and then they give him a good pummeling until the snowman is once again just snow. And then they act surprised that the snowman has disappeared.

Through it all I am on the sidelines taking pictures until the tears of laughter are running so hard I can't see through the viewfinder any more. The winters for us northern backyard horse people are filled with hard work—carrying buckets of warm water from the house, cracking ice in buckets frozen overnight, shoveling and shoveling and shoveling paths around the barn, slogging through deep snow, bundling up at 6 A.M., fingers and lips cracking from so much time outdoors. The snowman ritual has made winter just a tiny bit more tolerable for me, and I think for the horses, too!

Where has laughter made something more tolerable for you?

You Can Lead a
Horse to Water...

B ut you don't need a lot of gimmicks to make
him drink.

Look in any horse-related magazine or catalog (of
which there are hundreds) and you will find pages of
things that the catalog copywriters would like to make
you believe you can't have a horse life without. The
horse industry is full of people attempting to build a
better mousetrap.

For horses, the *mousetraps* are things like bits and sad-
dles and saddle pads and supplements. Many horse people
do spend their money on them. That's okay—most of
us get into hobbies like horses, golf, boating, or quilting
as much for the paraphernalia as the activity itself.
Collecting nice blankets and fly masks and halters and
lead ropes are all part of the fun of having a horse.

Some of the other stuff in the catalogs can be useful or they can just suck the money out of your wallet. Things like supplements have catalog copy that lead you to believe if you don't buy a tub of this and a tub of that and have it express mailed to you, your horse will die by Thursday. Like most aspects of life, simpler is better with horses, too. Especially when it comes to equipment.

For instance, some owners want to prevent their horse from holding his head too high when they are riding him. What are the options for solving this issue? Here's a short list:

You use a tie down—you literally tie the horse's head down from the bridle on his head to a strap on his chest that connects to the saddle on his back which forces him from being able to get his head up high. This also puts the horse in the "proper frame" that is typically desired.

You sell the horse and search around to find a new one who simply is not inclined to put her head high in the air. Of course, the new horse may instead buck like a champion rodeo horse or grab the bit and run away at full gallop and you have a new and equally as frightening issue to deal with. But it would provide an incentive to build a mousetrap to address that issue and maybe you'd get rich on the sales.

You could attach a piece of flat metal to your helmet that extends over the horse's head to make him think he has a roof above him so he doesn't put his head up high. (If this shows up in a catalog soon, I'd like some royalties.)

You could go to a clinic or find a good teacher so that you don't need to use exterior gimmicks to force your horse's head down, but instead learn better horsemanship that allows you to teach the horse what you want in a language he understands.

Again, the best solution seems clear to me—learn better horsemanship. No extra product needed, nothing to buy (except maybe someone's expertise in the form of lessons) and hang from a hook to collect dust when you find it doesn't work anyway. But when I look through the catalogs I get in the mail, I realize that what seems clear to me often is not based in reality. After all, if these products exist, someone must be buying them. But what these products do is *force* things to happen. The horse has no choices to make.

Often people resort to these gimmicks because they don't know how to teach a horse to lower his head or stand still or they don't know it's possible to teach the horse these things. With good horsemanship skills, you can put a simple bridle with a simple bit on your horse's head and a quality well-fitting saddle with a comfortable saddle pad on his back and climb on in sturdy boots with a small heel and an ASTM-certified helmet on your head and right there you have everything you need to do virtually anything to ride your horse.

What my horses have taught me about this forcing issue is that

> horses are not stupid, they can be taught everything you need them to know short of using an abacus to do your income taxes (no thumbs);

> forcing them into something seems like the easiest solution on the surface but it is far from the easiest solution in the long run. Forcing them makes them resentful and frustrated and in no way generates respect for the human.

Has someone ever tried to force you to do something? Did throwing you off the pier make you enjoy swimming? Did locking you in your room make you want to study? Being able to make decisions and think things through sets up an environment conducive to learning and puts the student in an open frame of mind whether the student is horse or human.

Making Life Sweeter

Having always found life extremely entertaining, I never thought life could get more enjoyable. And then I put horses in my backyard.

All animals entertain me—when I got two black kittens to add to the barn, at least an hour a day was used up watching the kittens play. I often sit in a lawn chair and let my goats loose; my plan is to read a book while they nibble and explore, but I usually do more goat watching than reading. And they are often trying to nibble on my book. I have snapped so many pictures of our two dogs, Dot and Dash, doing funny and cute things that we have a pictorial record of the entire decade of their lives so far. I don't have kids but I imagine if I did I would need a separate building to house the photograph albums.

But what I didn't realize was how endlessly fascinating the horses and their interactions would be. If I ever became wheelchair-bound, I would want to be wheeled every day to a place where I could sit and watch a few horses. Horses have taught me the power of observation. They *speak* in and respond to such fine nuances of body language that you can become a keen observer.

Having horses has become such a huge element in my life I can't imagine what I would do without them. My horse friends and I joke that we would be wealthy and have time on our hands if we didn't have horses. I feel lucky to have truly grown to know horses when I was in my thirties so if I do live a long life I will have had a lot of years to enjoy horses.

I hope everyone finds that thing that fulfills them—for my brother, it's running, for some it's golf, for others it's music or painting. Some people go from one thing to the next in search of something interesting. They buy all the requisite paraphernalia, take lessons, drop it in a year to eighteen months, and move on to the next thing. One of the things I really enjoy about horses is that there are so many aspects to it that you can get involved in—jumping, trail riding, driving, just plain horse care—that you don't have to think of it as one type of thing. And all the while you're giving a couple horses a good life. It is very rewarding and for me life is definitely sweeter with horses in the backyard.

Learning to Think
"Outside the Stall"

———◆◆◆———

The phrase "thinking outside the box" has become shopworn after years of use in the corporate world. But even after years of overuse, the concept is still of great importance and has good application to working with horses and improving our lives.

After the 9/11 terrorist attacks in the United States, there was much analysis of how such a massive undertaking could have escaped the radar of intelligence agencies not only in America but also around the world. Thomas Friedman, in a column in the *New York Times*, described the slip as "a failure of imagination" on the part of U.S. intelligence gathering. Little bits and pieces were known—that terrorist cells existed around the globe, including in the U.S., that the World Trade Center continued to be a target, and that democracy was not embraced and American influence (not to mention affluence) was not welcomed by everyone in the world. But even the top intelligence agencies did not pull these pieces together into the complex plot that was masterminded for that day.

When I read Thomas Friedman's column and those words "failure of imagination," I couldn't get them out of my mind. The gravity of the current state of the world fell with a thud from the pages of the *Times* op-ed section. They landed in my lap like an affection-starved cat—something that could make itself so heavy you can't brush it away, and every time you try it sinks its claws into your pant leg and clings. These words clung.

Thinking creatively can help us work through much more mundane things than terrorist attacks. My horses have taught me this. If I am trying to teach a young horse something, I need to think from the horse's perspective—way out of my own *box*. And when the approach I'm taking isn't working, I need to find a different approach.

For instance, early on in my relationship with my newest yearling colt, I decided that he must have had a frightening experience with a wheelbarrow since he was afraid of it. Perhaps it had been used to block the doorway to his stall when his original owner cleaned the stall, and the colt tried to jump over it and had a bit of a wreck. Or maybe he was chased with it. I will probably never know. He seemed less concerned about it when it was sitting still, but if I picked up the handles and moved the wheelbarrow, he would definitely run from it. And he was likely to kick at it too—not a desirable thing to the person holding the handles.

I tried to think of ways to get my colt more secure about the wheelbarrow and understand that it isn't going to hurt him. I was always careful to wheel it past him slowly so as not to concern him. This helped, but if the wheelbarrow made a noise bumping over a rock or a stump, he still would turn and face it with his eyes popped out of his head, or he would run away and kick.

Then I tried being careless with the wheelbarrow, going out of my way to have it make noise and letting the colt know that no matter what kind of noise the thing made, it wasn't going to come after him.

All of these things helped him get better about it over the first few months I had him, but I knew that in a crunch, he still could easily be frightened by the wheelbarrow, and I could get accidentally kicked. I didn't want him afraid of something so commonplace in the day-to-day care of my horses. So I turned to one of my teachers for an "out of the box" idea to take this further.

In herd behavior with horses, much is determined about pecking order based on who can move whom. The mover is higher up on the social ladder than the moved. My mentor suggested that I get someone to help me set up a situation where my colt thinks he is able to move the wheelbarrow. If my colt thinks that he can "move" the wheelbarrow, he may finally dismiss it as *beneath* him in herd status or it may, like a horse working a cow, make the wheelbarrow interesting instead of frightening.

Although I didn't get around to having someone help me, every time my colt showed interest or concern about the wheelbarrow, I took the opportunity to make it seem like he moved it. This was especially effective when I bought a large, light-colored wheelbarrow that made his eyes bug out! He came over to it in fascination and a little frightened and he immediately "made it move." Then he followed me everywhere, "pushing" the wheelbarrow out of his space. He has become less and less concerned about wheelbarrows ever since.

I am still very much learning, but I have been fortunate enough to have teachers throughout my life who have allowed me to think creatively. Finding people we can turn to who can help us imagine the possibilities can make life infinitely more interesting.

And maybe encouraging our children to think creatively and not trapping them in educational rituals but
embracing all learning tools can be the keys to creating a generation of adults who won't have to experience either the "failure of imagination" that leads to
devastating consequences or simply just plain boredom.

Tuning In to Your Inner Horse

When leading a horse on a lead rope, you don't ever want that horse to come to the end of the lead rope—you always want a loop in the lead rope, a "float" we call it. In fact, my farrier, Bill, gave me a great definition recently of a "halter broke" horse. Most people consider a horse halter broke if you are able to walk up to it and put a halter on. Bill's definition of halter broke is a horse that will never allow the slack to be take out of the lead rope—when you move, he moves. He is so in tune with your feel that you can *never* get enough ahead of him for the lead rope to tighten between you and him. There are perhaps a few dozen horses like this in the world and they are all owned by a dozen horsemen—but this lack of *truly* halter-broke horses is caused by a lack of horsemen who offer *feel* to a horse. Many of us can get our horses to this point for a day or two, but the horse will always step down to the level of his handler—in order to have a truly halter-broke horse you have to be a horseman with truly refined feel. Not impossible, but not easy and certainly something I aspire to.

So when you ask a horse to lead ahead, the horse who has been allowed to retain that innate feel will never let that slack go out of the lead rope. Those that have been insensitively handled will usually need to come to the end of the lead rope before they step ahead. Most need to actually be pulled on as well. Instead of "broke to lead" we jokingly call that "broke to drag."

How much feel a horse operates with is very much a product of how they are handled, especially in the first few years of their lives. While you can get an older "dull" horse to reconnect with this sensitivity, the handler has to be extremely sensitive to get much feel back with these horses.

Students new to the kind of horsemanship that I have studied find this feel thing the most elusive concept of all. It's a skill that can be taught to some degree, but it is almost impossible to define. The definition itself seems to come in the form of examples and exercises.

I watched a clinic by a man I had never seen give a clinic before. One of the students in the class asked for some help. She was working with her horse on the ground on a lead rope (i.e., not from the saddle) and her horse seemed to be getting grouchy about the things she was asking of him. The clinician flashed that knowing smile. He asked if she minded if he took her horse for a minute. When he took the lead rope from the woman, who we'll call Mandy, he asked her to stand over by the fence. We all assumed he was planning to work with the horse to "fix" whatever it was that was "wrong" with the horse and he wanted her out of the harm's way in case the horse got a little fired up.

She hadn't made three steps from the horse when the clinician said "Mandy, would you step over near the fence?" She kept going toward the fence, which is what she was already doing anyway, but when she was less than halfway there, the clinician said again, "Mandy, please go over the fence." Mandy finally turned around and held up her hands and looked frustrated. She *was* stepping over near the fence, why did he keep after her about it?

Of course, then it dawned on all of us, including Mandy. What this clinician was doing to her was the same thing she was doing to her horse. She was asking her horse to do something and while the horse was preparing to do it, she was still asking. And asking. And the horse, like Mandy did with the clinician, would get a little frustrated and cranky. Mandy was not being aware when working with her horse.

As Mandy learns more about feel, she will learn to recognize when her horse is even *preparing* to respond to her and she won't keep asking. Like many things, horses are great teachers of this—a cranky horse, Mandy found, isn't the most pleasant thing to have attached to you by a twelve-foot lead rope!

Retaining that feel is the most useful thing you will ever do with a horse. Although I am a million miles from where I'd like to be, with every horse I get, I have been able to retain that sensitivity a little bit better each time. The places where that sensitivity comes in handy are countless. And those places aren't all horse-related or even animal-related. You can gain by inches in communicating with your spouse or your children—maybe just because they aren't picking up their room this instant, they are doing what they need to do to prepare to pick up their room. Imagine the possibilities!

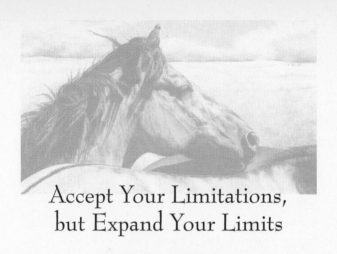

Accept Your Limitations, but Expand Your Limits

As I've mentioned, the first horse I got when I returned to the world of horses was a two-year-old gelding named Bud. The horse world is full of situations like mine—novice riders who get young horses whose needs far outweigh their new owner's skill level. Some horses are very forgiving and their kind and cooperative spirits allow them to fill in the gaps of the unskilled handler. Bud is not one of those horses.

It took a couple months of being kicked at and knocked around before I realized I was going to need a lot of help if this horse was ever going to understand the horse-human relationship. After I took him in a clinic to start him under saddle the need for assistance became even clearer—and that *I* needed to better understand the horse-human relationship!

I enlisted a couple local horse people to come by the barn where I was keeping Bud and give me a hand. We mostly got nowhere; he wasn't getting any more rideable than before. When I was on my own, I was still making regular imprints of my rear end on the arena floor.

I started to get desperate and off Bud went to a "professional horse trainer." He came back a little more rideable—the details of how that happened I never want to know—but the level of his rideability soon deteriorated back to my skill level.

Over subsequent years Bud and I went through many clinics together where I tried to up my skill level to a point where we could get along. It wasn't really happening; he was no fun and he was a dangerous horse for me. I had acquired a new horse so I put Bud on the back burner for several years. I did try to sell him— he is a beautiful mover when he moves out freely, which so far is only when a rider is not on his back. But he has a severe overbite that is unattractive and requires a bit of extra attention, especially as he gets older, and no one who was at the skill level he required wanted him.

My new horse was the complete opposite. I got Ruby at eight months old and she was forgiving, kind, and fun right from the start. She certainly had her issues but they were things I knew we could get over, not scary and dangerous things like the elevated, twisting bucks and rears that Bud displayed.

After a few years of confidence with Ruby under my belt and the acquisition of yet another young horse, I began to feel like it was time to get back to Bud. He was now over ten years old; it seemed a shame to have a big healthy horse in his prime languishing away doing nothing. Bud didn't seem to mind, but I had other ideas.

The first thing I did was sign him up for two clinics that season. The first clinic went well—the clinician kept everything on this side of the line representing my skill level. I had a few nice rides and was thrilled to discover how comfortable this horse is to ride— something I hadn't ridden him enough to discover in the nine years I'd had him!

Bud is renowned for his "honeymoon" phase—in his older years, he has been quite cooperative until he gets comfortable with the situation at hand. The second clinic was two or three weeks later. By then, this honeymoon phase of being ridden again was waning. The first day of the clinic went fine, the second day things began to deteriorate. The third day, I asked the clinician what to do and he asked if I wanted him to ride Bud for a few minutes. I never dismounted so fast (intentionally at least) in my life.

The teacher, a superb horseman, pushed Bud's limits and handled everything that came up. And some pretty wild things came up—bucking and a couple very impressive rears from this tall horse. I watched all of these antics and the clinician's ability to just hang in there—he never stopped chatting with us no matter what Bud pulled—and I went home anxiously wondering how on earth I was going to ride this horse the next day, the last day of the clinic. I just did not have the clinician's skill level.

Somewhere around two in the morning, I realized that the clinician had pushed Bud beyond his limits to give me another short honeymoon. Because of all the antics he allowed Bud to work through, I would be able to ride him the next day. And for every reasonable ride I got on Bud, I could make baby steps in my skill level in handling this difficult horse.

Instead of being afraid to ride him when I arrived at the clinic that day, I looked forward to it. I had been thinking I was wasting my money on this horse putting him through these clinics. But as always, I came back to the understanding that the horse is just the project in all of this, the person is the student. And any education I get is useful to me in all future riding of any horse.

I could look back on the clinician riding Bud and realize that I cannot ride him that way because my skill level is not that high. But I brought the horse to the clinic to expand my skill level, and that certainly happened. It's often hard, but we can learn a lot by pushing our limits. If there is a skill you want to learn or expand, find a way to push yourself beyond the point where you are comfortable. You may not remain at that level for long but you will settle back at least a notch or two higher than where you started.

Give Yourself Your Best Time of Day

My friend Linda has a couple geese. She works a regular office job and gets up very early in the morning to fit goose care into her schedule. Linda's geese are meticulously tended to—they always have fresh water, fresh bedding, and when she had several geese she added separating the sexes at night to her chores list. I tease her because she spends as much time tending to those geese as I do my herd of horses and two goats.

But I know why she does it. It is in our nature to get up early and get the day started. However, like everyone else, when the bed is warm and the dog or cat is snuggled at your feet and your husband is tucked up beside you, it takes some motivation to get out of bed when the stars are still shining. Linda and I are both so conscientious about our critters that it's motivation enough that they are out in the cold, dark barn anticipating our arrival to get us up and going.

My border collie, Dot, is just like me. When I get out of bed, she is ready to go despite the fact that she is still toasty warm from having slept at my feet on the down duvet all night. When Dot and I walk into my cavernous, three-story former dairy barn, my Arab mare gives a low nicker. The young colt in the stall below the barn lets out his high-pitched whinny. My gelding paces the corral, nickering with every turn. Ruby, my oldest mare, challenges her favoritism status every feeding time by standing at her feed tub and pawing the ground incessantly. Three barn cats swirl around my feet and two goat heads stick out from the stall gate to watch the proceedings and wait their turn.

Within a few minutes, all the horses are munching peacefully on their grain ration. By the time I'm done distributing hay, they are done with their grain and ready to head out from their stall or night pen. The older gelding is the boss of the group and every morning he plays Goldilocks, tasting each hay pile before settling down to one. The colt eats with my older mare, who occasionally gets tired of him stuck to her side and chases him away. He trots around testing who else might share with him, which is no one, and instead of eating alone at a pile he works his way back to his mare friend. The Arab mare trots around twirling her head and scooting here and there; she eats from a pile of hay for a few minutes but is often the first one to leave the hay and go to the slim pickings of grass beyond the barn.

In the meantime, Dot and I have our duties. The cats get fed a can of wet food, and Dot's job is to lick the plate clean when they are done. The goats, who are slow to really wake up, get hay and fresh water. We then start to clean paddocks and stalls. Ask any horse owner—manure cleaning may seem like a tedious job but the world's problems get solved during that quiet, mundane task. I empty the wheelbarrow, fill water tubs, and go inside for some breakfast of my own.

The time of the morning that I head to the barn changes with the seasons. When the light comes early, I'm out at daylight. I simply cannot stay in bed when the sun has risen, the birds are chirping, the chipmunks are chipping. But in late fall, winter, and early spring when darkness sticks around until after 6:30, I may get up at 5 A.M., but don't go out until after a cup of coffee.

My husband, who finds routine the best friend of Death, cannot understand how I can do this day after day after day. I cannot understand how I could not do it. I know it's not for him and that's okay. But for me the barn chores add structure to my day—especially since I work for myself and don't commute to an office. In the spirit of the old saying that if you want something done give it to a busy person, I get a lot done in the course of a day.

I spent a lot of years waitressing to make money—if you have the personality to do it, it is perhaps the best job that does not require a college degree to make you the most money in the least amount of time. I always felt that my waitressing experience taught me a lot about time management. I can map out a plan quickly in my head to get chores around the barn done with the least amount of steps: fill one water tub while I clean the corral, on my way out the gate, switch the hose to the other water tub and while that's filling, clean the manure in the outside pen, empty the wheelbarrow and on the way by to deposit it in its resting place, shut the water off.

But the best thing of all is that this routine has shown me that my best, most creative time of day is early in the morning. I love to sit at my computer and write while the darkness of the night lingers around me. Everything is peaceful and my thoughts flow unimpeded by the business of the day. The coffee is warm and I can feel it make its way through my system. Even if I don't face the window, I can feel the day starting to take shape and know when my creative thrust is coming to a close.

Does structure add to your own productivity? Try it for a couple of weeks. If early morning isn't for you, that's okay. Structure is the same whatever the time of day.

Transform Resistance with Persistence

Although the oldest horse, Bud, in my horse "herd" is a gelding and he is the head horse—he gets the first pile of hay to be tossed out, he gets the shelter if he wants it—my oldest mare, Ruby, is the boss. She tells everyone where they should stand, she determines if they go out to the farthest part of their pasture or if they come back to the barn. They all look to her for guidance throughout the day.

This means that my mare is not real happy to be taken away from her herd. If I load her in a trailer and take her away from the property, she is fine. But if I ride her on the trails at my own place, there are several turns in the trail where she puts up a fuss to go back to the barn. After all, who knows what kind of chaos is occurring back there without her? It doesn't help that the rest of the gang hollers for her at intervals. But we have established a ritual, Ruby and me, that involves some quiet contemplation for both of us and helps her settle before the ride or after.

I ride in my back woods mostly by myself and I do it for the peacefulness and simplicity—no need to hitch up a trailer and drive in a truck and all the fuss that goes with it. I could ride the same trail in the same direction at the same time of day every day and never get bored. Different wildflowers come and go, the New England woods in the autumn truly define the cliché "heaven on earth"—golds and reds and oranges carpet the trail and stand out against the dark tree trunks. The trail seems different when it is windy, different when it is raining, and achingly different when it is being covered up with falling snow.

If I could put words in my mare's mouth, they would probably be "yea, yea, yea, it's beautiful, let's get this over with and get back to the barn." The trail makes a big loop around the perimeter of our property, which means at some point the loop starts to head back to instead of away from the barn. After that point, if I decide to make a turn on a side trail, my mare fusses about that.

We've worked through this fussing—something known in the horse world as "barn sour" or "herd bound"—until it is a minor annoyance. Of course I wish I were skilled enough for it to have gone away all together or that I provided her with enough comfort and support for her to find me as enjoyable as she does her companions. We're not there yet, but she's only nine as of this writing, so hopefully we have many years ahead to keep working toward that.

To help work through this herd-bound issue, I don't avoid it. I make turnoffs intentionally, giving us the chance to work on it. If you avoid the things that are troublesome you will never make a breakthrough. With horses, this can mean the difference between really getting together with your horse or not.

For a while, our rides were a bit contentious. Ruby was constantly challenging me—"Do you really want to go that way? Just how badly? Badly enough to figure this move out?" Wham, she'd slam on the brakes and turn around. How about this one? And she'd back up twenty yards through stumps and rocks and shrubs. The thing with Ruby is that she never pulls stunts that are terrifically dangerous, just frustrating. She really is always challenging which one of us is in charge of the ride.

At some point I decided that we needed to not only address this issue head on but we needed some peace on our rides. Our property includes a quarter-acre area surrounded by a beautiful tall stone wall that ascends a small hill. At the top of the peak is a two-headstone cemetery where former owners of the property are buried—Elizabeth and Ephraim lived almost the entire 19th century. Their dual headstones are enclosed with iron rails set in classic New Hampshire granite posts.

The view from their gravesite is good—it is near the barn and house, which you can see looking northwest. To the west is the area we are attempting to make pasture—no small feat in rocky New Hampshire. Where there isn't a rock, trees are desperate to grow up. We cut the four acres five years ago and de-stumped half of it. The rest of the hardwood stumps have sprouted—while it is discouraging to watch it grow back, in the fall the area looks like an impressionist painting of dabs of brilliant color.

Ruby and I began to end our rides by taking a trip to the top of the hill to visit Elizabeth and Ephraim and enjoy their view. This was not a random decision—in order to get into the area, we had to go almost to the barn then turn right into the opening flanked by two huge granite pillars. Ruby needed to accept the fact that I wanted to turn off and go away from the barn one last time.

Of course, the first few times she made it clear that

this side trip was not on her agenda. Once I got her through the pillars, we walked along the edge of the stone wall and then turned left to start up the hill. We stopped at the graves, I asked Ruby to turn around, sometimes by moving just her front quarters, sometimes by moving just her rear quarters. Sometimes I asked her to back up a few steps, sometimes not. Then I would drop the reins and sit. At first I did this for a half minute, then a minute, then a couple minutes. Now I can sit at the top of that hill for ten or fifteen minutes. I look around at the property and Ruby does too.

This little "quiet time" ritual has become so important to me and seems so peaceful finally to Ruby that I've started doing it with my other young mare too. We have picked out our own spot—at the opening of our maple sugar house which overlooks a nice bird-filled swamp. I make sure these quiet places are near the barn where they can be somewhat near their pals and know that once quiet time is over, they aren't far from home. We can end our ride on a very peaceful note, no matter how things went out on the trail.

And in this way, working with horses, as usual, mirrors life in general. By facing the difficult things and considering them a puzzle to be solved instead of avoiding them we can find ways to work through confrontation and frustration to peace and cooperation.

Face the areas in your life that need work. Even though this may initially seem like too much trouble, remember that breakthroughs take time, patience, and persistence to happen.

Be Willing to Do the Adjusting

---◆---

People who have horses that give them problems
often recount all the things that are wrong with
the horse: he bucks, he's mean, she tries to kick me
when I enter her stall, she's so flighty. But horses just
live what they know. They do not stand around trying
to think up ways to make our lives miserable to be
spiteful—that lifestyle is strictly a human creation.
Horses are reactive, not proactive. They don't plan far
in advance, they live the moment.

So when something is going wrong with a person's
relationship with a horse, it is up to the human to do
the adjusting. The horse did not request that she be
owned by a specific person, locked in a box stall several hours a day, wear something tight around her belly,
and have a human climb on top of her and take her

places she doesn't really feel like going.

As the ones who put the horse in these situations, it is also our responsibility to do the adjusting when necessary. For instance, perhaps your horse seems grouchy when you feed her. Maybe you are always in a hurry when you go into your horse's stall and the horse feels she needs to be on the defensive—try slowing down!

Sometimes it's like that with human relationships as well. My friend, Edward, complains that he hasn't spoken with his teenaged children, who have lived with their mom since their parents' divorce when they were in elementary school, in weeks. They never call him and he isn't in the loop on their report cards.

I asked Edward if he ever called them. "No, I don't always have to be the one to call." Ah, but with teenaged children, you do. Edward is the adult; the onus is on him to create the relationship he wants with his children. Like horses, teenagers are basically victims of their circumstances. First, they didn't ask to be born, of course. In the case of divorce, they certainly didn't ask for their mother and father to live in separate houses. Until they are adults with their own life experience and values to draw on, their parents hold the responsibility of teaching them.

Sometimes even adults need other adults to do the

adjusting. Mrs. Smith proclaimed that she doesn't like Mrs. Ellis, who worked at the local post office. "She's a snob," Mrs. Smith said. "She never even says hello when I go into the post office." But when asked if she ever said hello first, Mrs. Smith said, "No, why should I?"

Well, maybe Mrs. Ellis is shy. Or maybe Mrs. Ellis thinks Mrs. Smith doesn't like her and therefore it would be inappropriate to say hello. Or maybe Mrs. Smith always comes into the post office like she is in a hurry and Mrs. Ellis doesn't want to make her late for whatever she is hurrying for by engaging in chitchat.

With a horse, most people just get rid of the horse and look for one that better suits them and that they don't need to do any adjusting for. Horses get run through sale barns regularly because of this. But if you are willing to look for ways that you might be able to adjust, then relationships of most any kind can be much more rewarding.

Shake Yourself Up Once in a While

❖

There is a quote that says that "the riding of a young horse is an excellent nerve tonic." Most of my horses are pretty young and so this quote rings very true to me. Two was the oldest age at which I bought all of my current horses; the other four were yearlings and under. I buy young horses for several reasons.

A lot of people don't want to buy youngsters because it is a long time before you can start riding them. So, they can be bought pretty cheaply. Since I just enjoy horses and am not looking for "prospects" for some highly competitive horse sport, I don't need to buy high-priced horses to add to my herd. The fact that they can't be ridden for a long while works fine for me; two riding horses are about as much as I can handle at any one time anyway.

An older (say seven years and up) horse that is selling cheaply is sometimes being sold because the owner has no time, but more likely the horse either has medical or soundness problems or difficult behavioral issues. While I was becoming more skilled in the fundamentals of truly good horsemanship, I didn't feel like I was capable of dealing with the kinds of things that could come up in a horse that some other person had put there. Not that I haven't caused behavioral problems with my young horses, but I know what they are and how they got there and I can deal with them and most often turn them around since they don't have a lot of history to draw on.

Now that I am more skilled, I feel ready to take on an older horse and am more confident that I can deal with much of what might come up. However, I will still always have a youngster around as long as I feel physically up for the task. I do usually take them to a clinic and have a skilled horseman help me put the first ride on them.

But even beyond those first rides, young horses keep you on your toes. And although I probably won't always be ready to put myself in that much danger, I do like to use my horses to push my comfort level.

You don't have to ride a young horse or run the Iditarod or jump out of an airplane, but there are many other ways for you to take yourself out of your comfort zone a little. Take a class in something that is unusual for you or volunteer with a group of people quite different form yourself.

My horses provide ways of shaking my day up. Although I have not yet done anything competitively, I am researching the dressage circuit and would like to get one of my horses to do a novice dressage test. To go out by myself into the dressage ring, formally salute to the judge, and complete a specific pattern will be a nice awareness exercise for someone like me who has spent the last twelve years riding in the back woods and in clinics where you are working on what you and your horse don't know, not showing off what you do know.

And once I take that first dressage test, I will never get the chance to do that again, ever. As the old saying goes, you never forget your first—and although the saying is typically used in regard to your first sexual experience, I believe that your first in anything is an experience that makes you more aware.

Some people have to change from thing to thing— skydiving one year, rodeo riding the next, motorcycling racing another—but I don't need to look farther than my horses to provide me with all the firsts I'll ever want: first time jumping, first time competitive trail riding, first time fox hunting. I will go from thing to thing to thing but for as long as I can, all of those things will probably involve a horse.

Look for those things to shake up your life a little. For some people, it has to be huge—pack your bags, sell your house, and move across the country. For others, it can be as small as changing the restaurant where you eat pizza every Friday night. What it is that shakes things up for you doesn't matter as much as doing it.

Avoid Gossip

I've read many things that tell you to simply not gossip. I think that is almost as futile as telling a human being not to eat. We seem to be designed to contrast and compare our own existence against our fellow humans. But seemingly innocent simple gossip can build into negative gossip pretty fast.

The horse world is full of gossip. People buy horses, sell horses, create problems with a horse and seek help, go on trail rides and do questionable things (or the rumor spreads that they did), win ribbons and questions about their competitive ethics arise, or their horse is lame and their caretaking skills are questioned.

Am I always outside the door of the gossip mill? Unfortunately not. It is something that I dislike about myself and constantly try to change. The first way to change is to define gossip for yourself.

For instance, whenever I find myself slipping into a discussion of sensational facts about another person, I stop and change direction, or even change the subject. I try to engage in conversation involving secondhand information only if it is relevant to something specific. For example, if I am planning a ride with someone and she suggests that I ask Anna to come along, I might find it appropriate to say that Anna fell off her horse and hurt herself and probably wouldn't be able to come—and I may only say that if Anna herself told me about the fall. If on our trail ride the conversation begins to deteriorate into that dark forest of gossip—e.g. "Anna really isn't skilled enough to ride the young horses she rides"—I will change the subject even though I may totally agree. I would only discuss that kind of thing if Anna herself was present. Then we could have an interesting discussion that wouldn't deteriorate into judging Anna's riding skills without her being able to join the conversation.

If I do engage in a gossipy conversation about someone, I try to be conscious of saying only things that I would say directly to the person about whom we are talking. And I try never to initiate such conversations.

You'll notice I say *try*. It is very difficult for the average person, even one consciously trying to avoid it, not to gossip during the course of the day. And each of us has someone who pushes our buttons enough to throw all of our self-imposed gossip rules out the window!

Are you a member of the gossip club? If so, and gossiping already leaves a bad feeling in the pit of your stomach, try avoiding it. If you hear yourself slip into gossip mode, change the subject. Avoid people that you commonly gossip with. See if you feel better about your interactions.

Some People Just Won't
Think Like You Do

---◆---

Ever since the first horse clinic I attended in 1991, I've come to totally believe in educating horses, not training them, as the best approach to horsemanship. Although it has taken me years to even come close to developing the skills to accomplish it, I quickly understood that the most appropriate way for me to work with a horse is to present myself to her with feel. That's it. I'd say all you need for equipment is a lead rope, but you don't even need that. If you have proven yourself reliable and consistent to the horse and are truly operating with feel, the energy between you and the horse becomes all the lead rope you need.

One of the reasons I believe that this resonated with me so profoundly is that I did not just stumble upon it, I was actively seeking it. Unlike many people I run across who profess to have been "doing this all along," my previous involvement with horses had not left me with any good feelings. Oh, sure, I had always enjoyed the smell of horses, had loved to feel their breath across my shoulder, to listen to them chomping on hay in the dim light of the evening barn, to watch them in a field. However, trying to interact with horses had left me frustrated and confused. I absolutely knew there had to be a better way, but at the time I knew absolutely no one whose horsemanship I truly admired.

In 1991, this approach to horsemanship, (though at the time they were calling it "natural horsemanship," that term eventually evolved into something else, so now I just refer to it as "good horsemanship") was just hitting the East Coast in the form of clinics. By the late nineties, clinicians were crawling all over the country. Many of these clinics were not much more than sideshows. The clinicians were showmen not horsemen. I won't name names, but the people who were getting the most publicity were the ones with giant marketing machines behind them. What people didn't know was that some of them did things like screening horses beforehand so that they could be certain that the ones they worked with in front of the audience would make them look good. That's okay, I guess, but the deceitfulness came in when they told the paying audience that they "had never seen the horse before this moment."

The horsemen I have studied with are real horsemen—able to deal with whatever horse or question they are handed. They are not afraid to "look bad"—although they are so skilled they rarely do. In other words, these horsemen are in it for the horse, not for the money or the prestige. They are horsemen (and women, but mostly men I'm afraid), not marketers. Of course they need to make a living, and some of them make a pretty good one, but their first and foremost concern is for the welfare of the horse and the horse's relationship with his owner.

As you can see, I have become pretty strongly planted in my beliefs. I have seen dozens of clinicians in action, have attended dozens of clinics both with my horse and just to watch. I have seen demonstrations by many clinicians who operate outside my way of thinking—using methods like clicker training or whip-like instruments called "carrot sticks," clinicians who use a set of games in their clinics and market those games well. I am not opposed to nor criticizing these methods. Whatever excites people to make a better connection with their horses that doesn't involve abusing the horse (physically or mentally), I'm all for. Horses are potentially dangerous animals that are tough for humans to understand and any help we can get is probably for the better. What works for me is not necessarily going to work for you and that applies to most everything, not just horses.

But despite all that, I am firmly committed to the way of good horsemanship I have based my horse life on. I would even venture so far as to say I think it is the best way, despite the fact that I don't believe it is for everyone—I have come to believe it works for every horse, but not for every person.

In believing this approach to good horsemanship to be the best, I spend my time developing my horsemanship. If people I ride with ask me what I would do about something, I tell them how I would approach it, and in the meantime I am approaching things with my own horses in the way I believe in. I don't rush to clinics on clicker training and walk around with a signboard saying that people who are using it are making their horses stupid. I am at home working on my own horsemanship, without a clicker on the property.

I write about it to help me think it through and to present my thinking to others to consider. The reader can choose to read what I write or not. If you engage me in conversation about horses and horsemanship, I will definitely approach the discussion from my way of thinking. My nature doesn't make me inclined to simply nod my head and not respond. However, in my own mind I am not trying to convince anyone of anything; if it comes across that way, it is by accident.

You simply can't convince someone of something like this. This philosophy of horsemanship itself tells us that—"Make the right thing easy and the wrong thing difficult" and "set it up and let it happen" are two sayings that are commonly tossed around in my horse world. If you want a horse to move in a certain direction, open that door and close the one you don't want the horse to go through. For those of us who have ever experienced a bird or a bat in the house, for instance, we've heard this advice before. We can get the bat out by beating it to death and tossing it out the door. Or, better I think, simply block all the doors and windows except one to the outside and get the bat or bird flying. It will almost certainly go out the open door.

What doors do you want open in your life? It is mostly up to you whether or not you walk through.

Be Sure You Want
What You Ask For

Horses thrive on consistency. Say a horse has been taught that when you pick up on the reins and pull back, it is a signal to the horse to stop. Then a new rider buys the horse. And some of the time, she pulls back on the reins, the horse stops, and she stops pulling. But some of the time, the rider pulls back on the reins, the horse stops, but this rider doesn't realize the she is continuing to pull back on the reins even though the horse has stopped. It won't take much of this inconsistency for the horse to start to have no idea what he is supposed to do when that rider pulls on the reins.

The same is true for handling the horse, not just in riding. For the most part, horse owners don't appreciate their horse dragging them around—so they teach them that when they are being led that there should be some slack in the lead rope. But for a handler who is not really aware, he may be gabbing with his friends while letting his horse graze on the lawn and not realize that the horse is dragging him around the lawn as the horse moves to new bits of grass—horses naturally roam while grazing so for the horse, this is what they do. And suddenly the horse can't tell the difference for when it's okay to drag the human around and when it's not.

Instances abound where consistency is key to the safety of being around horses. If you don't want your horses to crowd the gate when you come to feed, teach them not to crowd the gate and require that courtesy *every* time you go to feed. If you expect your horse to stand when you mount her, teach her to stand while being mounted then expect it *every* time—if she walks off just as you are putting the other foot in the stirrup, don't just dismiss it and figure you'll "fix" it next time. Start over and get it right. She won't know what you want if you don't ask her for it, every time.

Like leadership, consistency doesn't have to be militaristic or dominating or fear-inducing. Consistency is just plain respectful. Being consistent can create comfort, trustworthiness, and mutual respect in both human and horse relationships.

Be Humble

A show about the nature of horses was on public television recently. A woman who was working with a horse and rider began to talk about how humbling it is to work with horses. She said that just when you think you've figured it all out and consider yourself pretty sharp, the horse will come up with something you never even thought about. Horses can put you in your place pretty quickly.

I recently read Christopher Reeve's first book *Still Me*. Reeve became paralyzed when his horse refused a jump and he was propelled over the horse's head. Through a simple and unfortunate chain of events, Reeve landed on the top of his head on one of the jump's rails. Despite the fact that he had a helmet on, the impact broke his spine at one of the upper vertebrae.

Being a horse rider and having taken some jumping lessons, I was a bit reluctant to read too much about someone else's severe misfortune as a result of a fall from a horse. *Still Me* was several years old by the time I read it, but I became curious as a result of a lot of publicity regarding some amazing movement and sensation Reeve started experiencing (and continues to make progress with) that was unheard of for a quadriplegic of several years. Plus he had written a new book, *Nothing Is Impossible*, which was getting a lot of attention in the media.

So I picked up *Still Me* and as I read it, several things struck me. The first and foremost was that Reeve never once blamed his horse in any way. I found this truly admirable considering how dramatically his life was changed by the incident. In fact, a horsewoman with financial means and some political clout also noticed this, he tells toward the end of the book, and because of it she donated money to spinal cord injury research and helped him put together political support for this cause.

However, the earlier parts of the book did not reveal this depth of character. The type of person that Reeve described himself as being would have at least made mention of the no-good so-and-so that dumped him.

Another thing that struck me was that despite the

fact that Reeve recounted his strong attraction to horses and competitive riding, after the accident he never mentions having any desire to be among horses. And it occurred to me that the pre-accident Christopher Reeve was *not* interested in horses—just in competition.

I can't help but wonder if he had been as interested in the horses themselves as he was in *competing* with horses, he may have found this more humble part of himself earlier. Of course, many things in life are simply luck of the draw, and it would be ridiculous to suggest he would never have gotten hurt on a horse if he had been more humble at the time. Everyone who rides knows that one fall in the wrong place or landing the wrong way can be the difference between a couple bruises and something broken or worse.

But superficial pursuits lead to superficial attitudes. Christopher Reeve's discovery of humbleness was touching to listen to. In a *Fresh Air* interview a few years after his accident, he addressed this very topic. It was clear that in the years since his accident he had found the best of himself—and he sincerely encouraged other people to find it in themselves as well. Reeve has gone from someone I didn't find of much interest to someone whom I greatly admire.

Horses can make you humble. Not just because they are large impressive animals, which they certainly are compared to the size of humans. But they wear their emotions on their sleeves—they do not cheat, lie, or fake it. They lay it all out there and they can make you realize that they expect you to be trustworthy and consistent and a true leader.

In the years since I have returned to horses, I've learned that it's a lot to live up to. I accept and appreciate the challenge. And I encourage you to find that thing that makes you humble. The thing that makes you constantly assess your approach, your interactions with others, your life. Instead of doing all your examining at the end when you can do nothing to make changes, look back as you look forward, and continue to live in the present. Adjust where you can, find help when you need to, and be humbled—by horses or whatever you choose.

To Our Readers

Conari Press, an imprint of Red Wheel/Weiser, publishes books on topics ranging from spirituality, personal growth, and relationships to women's issues, parenting, and social issues. Our mission is to publish quality books that will make a difference in people's lives—how we feel about ourselves and how we relate to one another. We value integrity, compassion, and receptivity, both in the books we publish and in the way we do business.

Our readers are our most important resource, and we value your input, suggestions, and ideas about what you would like to see published. Please feel free to contact us, to request our latest book catalog, or to be added to our mailing list.

Conari Press
An imprint of Red Wheel/Weiser, LLC
P.O. Box 612
York Beach, ME 03910-0612
www.conari.com